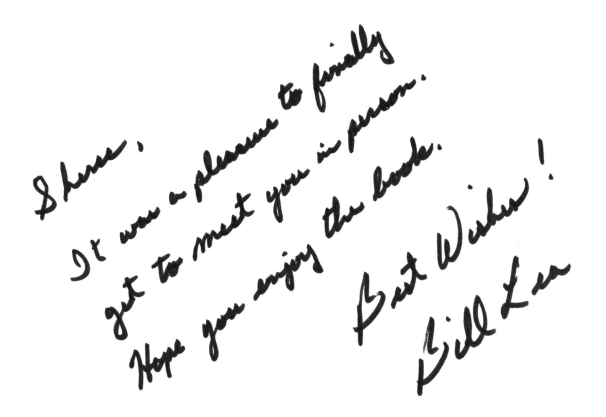

Shane,

It was a pleasure to finally get to meet you in person. Hope you enjoy the book.

Best Wishes!

Bill Lee

## Dedication

*To Klari, for all of the love and support you have provided over the years.*
*I love you and am forever grateful.*

*Above:* Female (black form) eastern tiger swallowtail.

*Right:* An efficient predator, a bobcat can find a variety of prey in the diverse habitats of the Smokies.

*Title page:* Though hidden among flowers and dense cover, this white-tailed buck remains alert.

*Front cover:* No other animal symbolizes the Great Smoky Mountains more than the black bear. There may be as many as 1,800 black bears living in the Park's half million acres.

*Back cover (top left):* Three young whitetails on the prowl during the autumn breeding season.

*Back cover (top right):* An inquisitive raccoon stands at the entrance of the hollow log it uses for a retreat.

*Back cover (bottom):* A white-tailed fawn wades a shallow stream in Cades Cove.

*Photographer's note:* The photos of bobcats and river otters were taken under controlled situations.

ISBN 1-56037-353-9
Photography © 2005 by Bill Lea
© 2005 Farcountry Press
Text by Bill Lea

For more information about our books write Farcountry Press, P.O. Box 5630, Helena, MT 59604; call (800) 821-3874; or visit www.farcountrypress.com.

Created, produced, and designed in the United States. Printed in Korea.

# GREAT SMOKY MOUNTAINS

*wildlife portfolio*

*photography and text by* **BILL LEA**

# INTRODUCTION

*by Bill Lea*

The sudden sound of snapping branches broke the silence of a mid-September day in Cades Cove. I eased quietly to the other side of the Loop Road, directly across from the Methodist Church, and peered into the forest. A large-necked whitetail thrashed his antlers among the brittle limbs of a toppled tree. With bulging muscles he raked his headgear back and forth, busting branches. After several minutes, he paused and, with a much calmer demeanor, rubbed his forehead gently across one of the stouter limbs numerous times. When finished, the buck methodically licked the exact same spot he had just christened with his forehead. He then stood motionless as if overcome by some hypnotic trance. Just about the time I thought the hostilities had ended, he flew into another tyrannic episode, tearing the treetop apart with mighty swings of his rack. As suddenly as it started, it stopped. The buck surveyed the damage in an apparently approving manner, let out a grunt, and then slipped into the woods like nothing ever happened. Quiet reigned once again.

Somewhat dumbfounded, I wondered what I had just witnessed. Having grown up in the city, I had few wildlife encounters in my repertoire of experiences. Yes, I loved the outdoors and had even graduated with a degree in forest resources and conservation, but, thirty years ago, this was all new to me. I knew one thing—I felt an extraordinary adrenaline rush watching that big buck exhibit what I would later learn to be rutting or breeding-season behavior. Little did I know that this first encounter with a deer in rut would inspire a lifelong passion for observing and photographing wildlife in the Great Smoky Mountains.

Capturing images of wild-life on film is a fabulous pursuit in itself, but to do so in the Smokies adds a totally new and exciting dimension. At 200 to 300 million years old, the Great Smoky Mountains once may have loomed as tall as the present-day Rocky Mountains. However, time and weather have rounded and lowered the Smokies' mountaintops.

A white-tailed buck wreaks havoc upon the brittle branches of a fallen tree.

The Smokies do not flaunt a majestic peak like Alaska's Mt. McKinley, yet they stand in a class all their own. Abundant moisture, rich soils, and elevations ranging from 875 feet to 6,643 feet combine to produce an amazing diversity of plants and animals. They certainly deserve the United Nations' designation as an International Biosphere Reserve. For example, with more than 100 different kinds of trees, the Smokies' half million acres of mature forests showcase a greater diversity of tree species than all of Europe. Herbaceous plants and wildflowers are equally diversified and prolific. As former park naturalist Arthur Stupka once wrote, "Vegetation to Great Smoky Mountains National Park is what granite domes and waterfalls are to Yosemite, geysers are to Yellowstone, and sculptured pinnacles are to Bryce Canyon National Park."

This vast flora provides a variety of habitat for a wide range of fauna. Of course, this same dense vegetation makes it difficult to see a lot of the wildlife that inhabits the Smokies. It is relatively easy to observe animals in the open plains of a national park like Yellowstone, but not here in the Great Smoky Mountains. Yes, the mountain peaks, ridges, and "hollers" host a considerable array of critters, but seeing them takes knowledge, patience, and a bit of luck. Cades Cove and Cataloochee Valley, with their open meadows, are the exception. Today the Park's maintenance of the former agricultural fields of mountain farmers provides visitors an easy opportunity to view white-tailed deer in Cades Cove and the newly reintroduced elk in Cataloochee.

Yes, elk once roamed the woodlands of the Smokies. Over-hunting and loss of habitat brought about their demise probably sometime prior to 1800. However, through the tireless efforts of Great Smoky Mountains National Park personnel, the Rocky Mountain Elk Foundation, and other organizations and private individuals,

*Park visitors seldom catch a glimpse of the elusive gray fox. Unlike the red fox, a gray fox can climb a tree if needed.*

elk were reintroduced into Cataloochee Valley on the North Carolina side of the Smokies in 2001. Nearly all of the elk inhabiting the Smokies today bear radio collars and ear tags as part of the ongoing study. Currently, the reintroduction project exceeds all expectations, although no final decisions will be made concerning its ultimate success until the study concludes five years following its inception. Absent for more than two centuries, the distinctive sound of elk bugling resonates through the forests of the Great Smoky Mountains once again.

The National Park Service's preservation mission often includes reestablishing native species that have been eliminated as a result of human influence. In addition to the reintroduction of elk, Great Smoky Mountains National Park has successfully reintroduced peregrine falcons, several species of small fish, and river otters. I will never forget the rainy day I observed four otters enjoying what appeared to be a game of tag along the banks of the Little River. I know of no other animal as playful as otters, and I know of no better place for otters to play than the Great Smoky Mountains.

Of course, no animal symbolizes the Smokies more than the black bear. Much interest and mystique surrounds this normally shy and reclusive inhabitant of the forest. Of all the animals people most want to see when they visit Great Smoky Mountains National Park, without question the black bear is the most popular. Unfortunately, some visitors seem to lose all common sense when they see a bear in the Park. Black bears should not be approached but observed from a distance. We need not fear bears, but we should maintain a healthy respect for their strength and wildness.

I most often see bears in the Smokies when they are feeding in treetops. In August they may be seen plucking the ripe fruit from black cherry trees, and in September they may be

A white-tailed doe and her fawn find relief from the summer heat in a Smoky Mountain stream. They cannot, however, escape a few pesky flies.

found in massive oaks munching on acorns. Once the accessible nuts are consumed, it leaves only those growing on the end of branches too small to support the weight of a big bear. Not to be denied, a bear will often break off good-sized limbs by mouth and then drop them to the ground. When a number of such limbs have accumulated, the bear will climb down the tree and then leisurely—and literally—consume the fruits of its labor.

Great Smoky Mountains National Park provides more than 800 square miles of primarily undeveloped, contiguous forest habitat. This is perfect for bears. Population studies conducted in 2000 indicate there may be as many as 1,800 black bears residing in this vast sanctuary. That is approximately two bears per square mile—maybe the densest population of black bears in all of North America. Surprisingly, in 1934, when the Park was established, black bears had become quite scarce in the Smokies. Today, bear sightings from even heavily traveled roads are relatively common. From my car I once observed an adult bear easily climb 40 to 50 feet and completely disappear into a small opening near the broken-off top of an old tree—black bears can squeeze into surprisingly small dens. The opportunity to witness such behavior attracts many visitors to the Smokies each year.

On the opposite end of the spectrum, the Great Smoky Moun-tains represent a haven for salamanders. It has been said that

*An American robin strikes a regal pose in a crabapple tree.* PHOTO BY RICHARD DAY

if we could weigh all of the salamanders in the Park and then weigh all of the black bears, the salamanders would outweigh the bears! The Park's abundant moisture (some elevations may receive 100 inches of rain during wet years), high summertime humidity, and more than 2,100 miles of streams provide some of the best salamander habitat anywhere. At least thirty species have been identified here. One species, the red-cheeked salamander, occurs nowhere else in the world. These small creatures escape the eye of all but the most discerning Park visitors.

The Great Smoky Mountains are home to approximately 66 different species of mammals, 200 varieties of birds, more than 80 types of reptiles and amphibians, 50 native fish species, and in excess of 3,000 kinds of moths and butterflies. Throw in the stunning mountain scenery, vast forests (of which 20% are considered old-growth), and a cornucopia of wildflowers and it easy to understand how a person could spend a lifetime photographing wildlife in such a setting. The opportunities are limitless. I have enjoyed more than a quarter century of this pursuit and hope to do the same during the next twenty-five years.

*Left:* A raccoon emerges from its den. Decay in old-growth trees creates ideal habitat for den-dwelling birds and mammals of the Smokies.

*Below:* The ability of some species to blend with their surroundings often means the difference between life and death. Camouflaged against the bark of a black cherry tree, this moth will probably escape the eyes of any predators, as well as most Park visitors.

While walking through crunchy autumn leaves, this black bear suddenly made a U-turn. Whether the young bear heard or smelled its prey I do not know, but it immediately shoved its nose into the depths of a yellowjacket nest. The angry wasps attacked the intruder, but their relentless stings never penetrated the bear's thick hide.

*Above:* The colorful blue jay resides year round in the Smokies.
PHOTO BY RICHARD DAY

*Left:* A bull elk looks and listens for any potential threat in the dense morning fog of Cataloochee Valley. All of the recently reintroduced elk wear radio collars so researchers can track their movements.

A coyote on the prowl.

*Left:* A Canada goose rests in an open field in Cades Cove but remains alert for potential predators like the coyote.

*Below:* A gray squirrel pauses for a quick look before resuming its nest-building chores.

*Left:* A wild and woolly gaze from an immature screech owl.

*Below:* The furry creatures and winged critters receive a lot of attention in most parks. However, an entire world of fascinating flora and fauna awaits the attentive eyes of visitors to Great Smoky Mountains National Park. Here, a small snail inches its way amid moss, lichen, and tiny plants.

A sleepy bear lifts its head from the comfort of a carefully constructed day bed.
It may have heard a sound as subtle as a snail on the move.

Two young bucks gently engage in the fine art of sparring. Such youthful play
hones the skills needed to establish dominance in later years.

A cottontail rabbit hunkers down in the forest shadows of the Tremont area. In many years of photographing wildlife in the Smokies, I have only seen a handful of rabbits.

*Left:* Fairly common in summer, pine warblers will occasionally spend a winter in the Smokies.
PHOTO BY RICHARD DAY

*Below:* More than eighty species of reptiles and amphibians live in the Smokies. This is an eastern painted turtle.

A black bear's fur can reach a temperature of more than 180 degrees Fahrenheit in direct sunlight. Lounging on a shaded rock is one way for a bear to beat the summer heat.

Mutual grooming by sibling fawns and between does and their offspring occurs frequently among white-tailed deer. Wet hair from rain or morning dew often dictates the need for such attention.

A raccoon explores the edge of a pond in Cades Cove. Shallow depressions hold water on a seasonal basis and provide ideal habitat for a variety of wildlife.

*Right:* A young bear finds a comfortable perch in the crotch of a tree. Most visitors to Great Smoky Mountains National Park hope to see a black bear more than any other animal.

*Below:* The drumroll of wings beating on a hollow log sounds like a motor slow to start but then quickly accelerating. The breeding ritual of the ruffed grouse reverberates throughout the forests of the Smokies. Here, a grouse stands poised to fly.

A white-tailed doe "in flight."

*Above:* A distant sound draws the immediate attention of a bear and her two cubs.
A mother bear will do almost anything to protect her offspring.

*Right:* This scene of a tufted titmouse with its rust-colored flank could pass for a decorative ornament on a Christmas tree.

PHOTO BY RICHARD DAY

*Far right:* Winter can be a lean time for bobcats, as well as other animals in the Smokies.

How does one measure the aptitude of a black bear? Indications of intelligence include the bear's curious nature and having the heaviest brain per body length of any land mammal. If you want to know for sure, simply observe or ask people who spend a lot of time with bears.

This cub seems to feel as snug and cozy in a tree as we do in our own beds. Slightly curved claws enable black bears to climb trees. With much longer curved claws, grizzly bears cannot climb trees. All bears in Great Smoky Mountains National Park and in the East are black bears.

*Above:* A tiny box turtle peers from its protective armor.

*Above:* A seemingly translucent red-spotted newt pauses mid-stride while crossing a small patch of bright-green wind-swept moss. The humid environment of the Great Smoky Mountains creates near-perfect habitat for a large population of salamanders.

*Right:* A white-tailed buck bears his deep-red coat amidst the lush vegetation of Cades Cove. A deer's summer coat has more individual hairs than its winter coat. The more numerous but finer summer hairs provide protection from biting insects.

Many animals benefit from the dark recesses of the Smokies' forests. This raccoon's ever-groping paws searched the bottom of a shallow stream and found a variety of items to its liking.

A bobcat hides among the forest shadows, perhaps waiting for its next meal.

The deep-blue indigo bunting is actually black in color, having no blue pigment. Light diffracted through the feathers makes this unique bird appear blue. PHOTO BY RICHARD DAY

The shallow water of a sinkhole in Cades Cove reflects the brilliant blue sky above. Sinkholes form when acidic water dissolves the limestone base and the ground subsequently collapses, creating a depression. This geologic process often produces wetland habitat that benefits a variety of fauna. Deer frequently visit sinkholes in search of specific plants growing in these wet environments.

*Left:* The color and shape of a preying mantis mimics the stems and leaves of plants. Predators often blend in with their surroundings so they can ambush their prey. This particular preying mantis had just consumed the last morsels of a moth when I spotted it.

*Facing page:* A black bear nuzzles her cub. First-time mothers often give birth to a single cub. A very close bond develops and the two bears are nearly inseparable for the first year and a half. Black bears give birth every other year at best.

*Below:* A butterfly sips the sweet nectar from an ironweed blossom.

*Left:* A white-tailed buck grabs some quick nourishment during the height of the energy-consuming breeding season.

*Facing page:* Extremely social animals, three otters collapse in a heap for a quick break. Thanks to reintroduction efforts by the National Park Service, otters once again inhabit the rivers and streams of the Great Smoky Mountains.

*Below:* A gray squirrel eyes the world below from its roost on a limb above Cades Cove Campground. Such squirrels can be spotted frequently in and around the campgrounds of the Smokies, where they have become accustomed to human activity.

*Left:* A bachelor herd of whitetails graces a summer meadow against the scenic backdrop of the Great Smoky Mountains. The National Park Service maintains the fields developed by farm families who settled in Cades Cove during the 1800s. Today visitors and wildlife reap the benefits.

*Below:* Surprisingly, I rarely encounter quail in the seemingly ideal habitat of Cades Cove. When I do, the sound of their unique *"bob white, bob white"* call adds a touch of elegance to an already exquisite setting.

*Left:* A southern green stinkbug crawls toward the bright red berries of an autumn dogwood. Don't touch this odoriferous insect; there is a reason for the "stink" in its name.

*Below:* A male and female cardinal perch on a pine bough. The birds' brilliant red plumage seems to imitate a Roman Catholic cardinal's vestments.   PHOTO BY RICHARD DAY

In the Great Smoky Mountains, much of a bear's diet consists of fruits and nuts. The bright-red berries of a mountain ash tree will help this bear gain the weight needed to survive another winter.

A white-tailed
doe and her
fawn pose for a
portrait in the
middle of
Abrams Creek
in the heart of
Cades Cove.

River otters and a host of other wildlife benefit from the more than 2,100 miles of streams, creeks, branches, forks, prongs, and rivers in the Smokies.

*Above:* A young raccoon clings to the upper branches of a small tree where it has taken refuge along Sparks Lane in Cades Cove.

*Right:* White-tailed yearlings groom one another under the watchful eye of their mother. The hollow hairs of their winter coats provide near-perfect insulation, allowing frost to form on their backs. Warm sunlight melts it, thereby requiring a little hair touch-up.

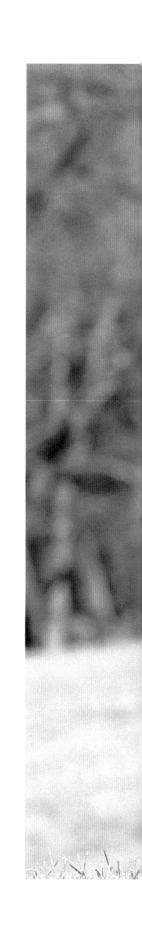

A small flock of Canada geese takes flight as the sun disappears behind clouds to the west. It still seems strange to hear their honking in the Smokies. I do not remember seeing geese in my earlier years photographing here.

With a certain sense of urgency, a black bear searches for autumn acorns. A bear may feed up to twenty hours in a twenty-four-hour period during the fall season. Bears can lose up to a third of their body weight while sleeping in their winter dens.

*Above:* A mourning dove withstands the chill of a Smoky Mountains snow.

*Above:* This gray squirrel is retrieving the acorns it buried a few months earlier. Its keen sense of smell helps it locate the nuts through layers of soil and snow. The un-recovered nuts will grow into trees, filling forests of the future.

*Right:* A December fog spreads an icy glaze on grass, twigs, and limbs. The deer appear oblivious to the beauty of the surrounding winter wonderland. I would not trade a moment like this in Cades Cove for anything.

*Right:* The Smokies are home to the red-cheeked salamander. These salamanders do not have lungs and must breathe through their mouth and skin. These unique creatures are found only in the Great Smoky Mountains.
PHOTO BY STEPHEN KIRKPATRICK

*Facing page:* A buck stands in a field of grass topped with remnants of a morning's frost. In the many years I've spent photographing white-tailed deer in the Smokies, I have encountered a few individuals with an almost black-colored face. The facial hair of this particular buck grew lighter in subsequent years.

*Below:* Whenever I hear the distinctive sound of a pileated woodpecker, I always think of the Smokies. Their haughty laughter often echoes through the old-growth forests. This woodpecker hammered the tiny stump for nearly twenty minutes as it searched for insects. Powerful blows sent woodchips flying in all directions (many of them are visible in the foreground).

*Right:* A white-tailed buck consumes an assortment of delicacies on a foggy morning in the Smokies. A deer must always keep a watchful eye for potential predators—although a healthy buck like this one has nothing to fear from a red fox.

*Below:* A red fox on the prowl in Cades Cove. Small mammals, rodents, and birds represent the main entrées on a fox's menu. It has little interest in a full-grown deer.

*Left:* I had been photographing deer in Cades Cove and was about ready to call it a day when I suddenly spotted a bird I had never seen. I took a quick shot, and in a moment it was gone. From the photo, it was identified as a bobolink, a unique bird known for its joyous, bubbling song.

*Below:* A ruby-throated hummingbird sits on her tiny, lichen-covered nest. Compare the size of the nest to the nearby leaf. Hummingbirds commonly lay two eggs, each about the size of a pea. At maturity the bird will reach a length of about three inches.

Black bears always seem to be moving, so I felt fortunate to capture this moment on film. Something in the distance caught the bear's attention, stopping it dead in its tracks for just a moment. Most successful images are simply a matter of luck.

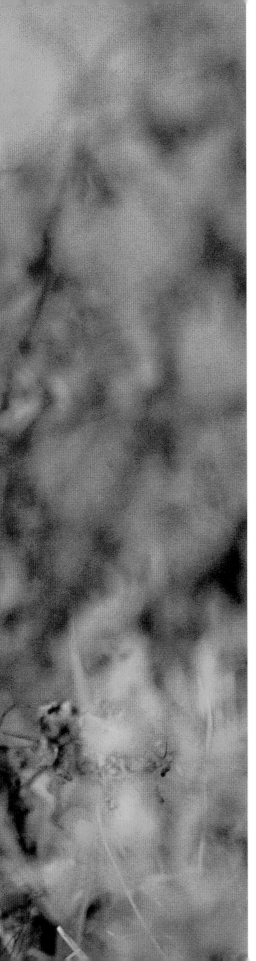

*Right:* A grasshopper climbs to the top of a ten-foot-tall yellow-flowered wingstem in search of a meal.

*Left:* A bobcat kitten peers anxiously from its protective cover. When so young and vulnerable, survival often depends upon staying quiet and concealed.

*Below:* Approximately 120 species of birds nest in the Smokies. Here, three baby robins have outgrown their nest. They will all take their first test flight by day's end.

*Right:* A turkey puffs up and struts his stuff in an effort to gain the affection of a hen. She appeared totally unimpressed with the tom's advances and continued to preen.

*Below:* A white-tailed doe takes in the sights, sounds, and smells of her fall surroundings.

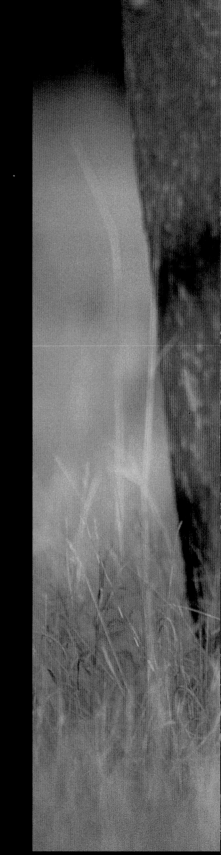

*Above*: The normally reclusive black bear has an extremely keen sense of smell and excellent hearing. This bear rests behind a cluster of black-berries that will soon be ripe enough to eat.

*Left*: Researchers believe black bears have good close-up vision and can see color. There appears to be more uncertainty about bears' long-range vision.

*Right*: In autumn, a black bear may travel great distances in search of the food it needs to survive winter. In the Smokies, acorn production varies from year to year. I have observed bears feeding on walnuts in November during years of acorn shortages.

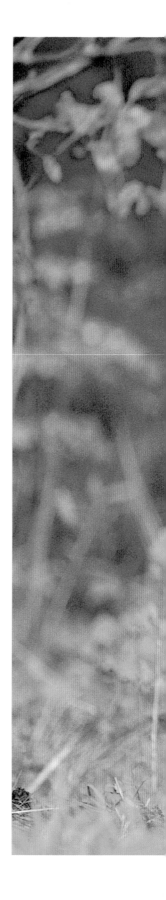

Two bull elk cross paths during the autumn rut. The significant difference in antler size assures the bull on the right his dominant position without need of aggression. Bright-yellow ear tags help researchers identify specific individuals as part of the five-year experimental elk reintroduction project.

*Above*: I frequently hear the familiar *"whoo whoo whoo cooks for youuu"* call of the barred owl, but I seldom see the source. I was lucky to find this particular owl in a hemlock tree within 100 feet of the Loop Road in Cades Cove.

*Right*: A raccoon pauses long enough to create a mirror image in a still pool in Rowans Creek.

*Left*: A black bear rests comfortably in the tangled branches of a red maple tree. The bear spent nearly five minutes breaking limbs with its powerful jaws to make the perfect day bed.

A gray fox pauses at the edge of the woods near day's end. It had been hunting for grasshoppers in the field for nearly an hour. Wherever it walked a grasshopper would jump, causing the fox to take off in a new direction.

A river otter takes a brief break from its grooming chores.
This charming face needs no work in my estimation.

*Right:* An autumn bobcat holds a perfect pose while on the lookout for possible prey.

*Below:* A moss-covered rock serves as an ideal pillow for this white-tailed fawn.

*Right:* Even a black bear has to take a break now and then. I once saw a bear jump to its feet from such a break when a chipmunk startled it from behind.

*Below:* A chipmunk buries a small nut in preparation for the winter ahead.

Left: In the summer, a dominant white-tailed buck will often pair with a subordinate deer and feed together for the safety of both. Here, a slight noise from the right caught the attention of both deer. The buck on the left looks and listens intently. Only mildly concerned, the deer on the right simply turns his ears back as he watches for a reaction from his cohort.

Below: With a sleepy look, a groundhog stands upright to survey its surroundings.

*Left:* A Canada goose takes a sip from a small flow of water in a Cades Cove field. A bear walked through the woods a few hundred yards away, but the thirsty goose never noticed.

*Below:* A good-natured striped skunk pauses from its relentless search for food. Some of the skunks I have encountered have narrow white stripes running down their backs, while others are nearly covered with white hair. This seemed to be a particularly handsome skunk.

This black bear almost passionately hugs the decaying log it tears apart in search of tiny delicacies. A long sticky tongue darts in and out, snatching various insects as they appear. It takes a lot of ants, termites, and such to fill a hungry bear.

A coyote tunes in on a barely audible sound from deep beneath the snow. Mice, moles and voles make up a substantial portion of a coyote's diet, but of course it would also consider an "entrée a la songbird" if given the chance.

*Right:* A purple finch winters in the Smokies.

*Below:* Fluffed-out feathers provide insulation and help this goldfinch control its body temperature.

*Right:* A white-tailed buck reaches up to browse on leaves of a tulip tree.

*Far right:* A tulip tree limb provides the perfect lounge as this raccoon hangs out on a summer day.

*Right:* Black vulture preparing for flight from the top of a dead tree or snag. Notice the den opening—it was excavated by a woodpecker and has probably served as a nesting place for various occupants over several seasons.

*Left:* It is almost breeding season for whitetails in the Smokies. When a buck smells a doe in estrus, he brings the odor directly to his nostrils by tilting his head back and curling his lip upward. This intense reaction is commonly referred to as lip-curling or flehmening.

*Below:* A red squirrel begins the arduous task of peeling a walnut nearly a third its own size. In the Southern Appalachian Mountains, red squirrels are often called "boomers."

*Right:* The playful antics of a black bear cub serve a vital role in developing the muscles and coordination needed to survive the rigors of life.

*Facing page:* Even as a youngster, a cub knows to be ever watchful.

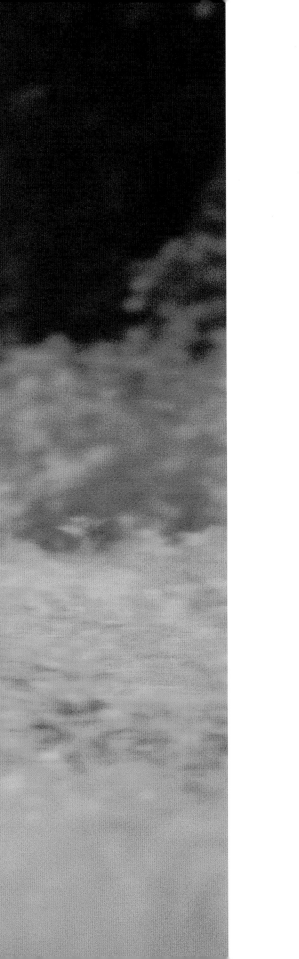

*Above:* A male black bear postures himself with arched back and extended legs. He approaches another male in this manner at a slight angle in an effort to appear larger and more dominant. The bear hopes it will eliminate the need for direct confrontation, thus avoiding possible injury.

*Left:* I am always amazed at the speed and grace of the white-tailed deer, especially on such long and slender legs.

*Above:* A young opossum clings to a tree, using its tail to achieve the perfect balance.

*Right:* Warm sunshine will soon send this white-tailed deer, feeding in a frost-covered meadow, to the shadowed forest in the background. Note the extra tine extending from the base of the buck's right antler.

*Above:* A white-tailed doe stretches to reach the leaves of an overhanging branch while a buck grazes in the shadows behind her.

*Facing page:* The approach of another bear sent this youngster racing to the base of a tree—ready to climb. If the intruder takes a step or two closer, the yearling bear will scurry up the tree to the safety of a lofty perch.

*Facing page:* I encountered this extraordinary bear in Cades Cove. She had only three legs but was successfully raising her two cubs. I only saw her once and do not know how she lost her front right leg.

*Below:* In September, a dominant bull elk gathers a harem of females as part of the breeding season ritual. He works hard at keeping the group together and fending off rival bulls. Notice the calves do not have collars or tags. They were born in the Smokies as part of the elk reintroduction project.

*Above:* Photos provide the opportunity to study the fine details that often go unnoticed during the excitement of field observations. Here, long white whiskers stand in stark contrast to the short tufts of black hair on the tips of the bobcat's ears.

*Left:* In today's world, antlered deer seem to receive most of the attention, but a doe possesses an inherit beauty difficult to describe in words. Notice the elegance of her big brown eyes along with the rest of her delicate facial features.

A black bear cub plays hard and sometimes needs a little support to make it through the day. This cub takes a well-deserved break and gets the assistance it needs from a nearby tree.

Look closely—here is a mother bear with her three cubs. This image defines the term "family tree."

*Above*: The reds of nature come in various forms. The red-tufted head of a pileated woodpecker compliments similar tones of a flowering dogwood's autumn leaves.

*Right*: A turkey bellows a distinctive gobble to announce his presence. The colors of his head will change in correspondence with his mood. A vivid red waddle and a light-blue head suggest this bird might be in love.

*Left*: A black bear tests the air for various scents against a backdrop of autumn red leaves. Under the right conditions, bears have been known to pinpoint a food source several miles away.

Autumn gold—the Great Smoky Mountains represent a treasure of color and wildlife. Here, a white-tailed buck shows his "white tail" while pursuing a doe through a field of golden grass.

A white-tailed buck chews his cud under the golden canopy of a fall forest along Rowans Creek in Cades Cove. It doesn't get much better than this for a nature photographer.

*Above:* A white-tailed buck reveals his autumn antlers. I have observed deer eat the nutrient-rich strands of velvet that often hang from their newly exposed headgear. As the breeding season approaches, a buck instinctively knows he needs all the nourishment he can consume.

*Left:* The mischievous look and energy of these two cubs spell double trouble.

*Above*: Summer insects can be relentless in their harassment of black bears and other wildlife.

*Right*: There is nothing worse than the constant buzzing of biting bugs around one's ears and face. This bruin couldn't "bear it" any longer.

*Far right*: Regardless of such distractions, a bear must always remain on full alert for potential danger.

In wildlife photography, the eyes always tell the story. Behind the contemplative look of a black bear there exists an intelligence that humans have just begun to understand

The look in this baby screech owl's eyes seems to convey
a certain sense of bewilderment.

A white-tailed buck seeks the protective cover of a Smoky Mountain forest to lessen the impact of driving snow pellets. The deer looks forward, but both ears turn back to detect predators that may approach from the rear.

A yearling bear descends an old-growth sycamore. Bears climb headfirst up a tree and feet first down a tree.

*Right:* This is probably a two-and-a-half- to three-and-a-half-year-old bear. Young bears often grow into their oversized ears.

*Facing page:* The cycle of life continues as the white-tailed doe eats the grass that produces the milk that sustains the growth of her offspring. Notice the fading spots of this late summer fawn—her nursing days will soon be over.

*Right:* Coyotes have been migrating east for a number of years and have only recently made their way into the Smokies.

*Facing page:* The National Park Service will not attempt to remove this newcomer since it arrived naturally.

*Below:* The coyote fills a portion of the niche left vacant by the loss of other predators.

*Below:* Just outside its den, a groundhog is on the lookout for possible danger. The large field adjacent to the Mountain Farm Museum at Oconaluftee is one of the best places to view groundhogs in the Park.

*Above:* A monarch butterfly rests on grasses wet with dew in Cades Cove. It is hard to fathom how such a delicate creature can migrate more than 2,500 miles to the Mexico mountains for winter.

*Right:* Shading one eye with its tail, a gray fox curls up on the forest floor for a well-deserved nap after a morning's hunt.

*Above:* A white-tailed fawn enters the world nearly odorless, so as not to attract predators. The newborn's only escape from predation depends upon maintaining a low profile. Camouflaging spots, the instinct to remain motionless, and a bit of luck often determine a fawn's fate.

*Left:* The dominant whitetail dictates when grooming is appropriate. A few minutes after this photo was taken, the subordinate buck tried to initiate similar behavior and received a flying hoof of discipline to his nose in response. Size and might makes right in the world of the whitetail.

*Following page:* A black bear cub surveys its surroundings, totally oblivious to the good fortune he has of living in the beauty and wonder of these Great Smoky Mountains.